T0194875

From Working
in the
Cotton Fields
to
Working
in
His Kingdom

JAMES FORTINBERRY

WESTBOW
PRESS®
A DIVISION OF THOMAS NELSON
& ZONDERVAN

WestBow Press books may be ordered through booksellers or by contacting:

WestBow Press
A Division of Thomas Nelson & Zondervan
1663 Liberty Drive
Bloomington, IN 47403
www.westbowpress.com
844-714-3454

Scripture taken from the New King James Version®. Copyright © 1982 by Thomas Nelson. Used by permission. All rights reserved.

ISBN: 978-1-6642-5519-7 (sc)
ISBN: 978-1-6642-5520-3 (hc)
ISBN: 978-1-6642-5521-0 (e)

Library of Congress Control Number: 2022900535

Print information available on the last page,

WestBow Press rev. date: 01/28/2022

CONTENTS

PREFACE

This account of my life and ministry is an attempt to communicate to the reader what a wonderful God we serve. Since it is an autobiography, the terms *I* and *me* will occur often. It may seem like bragging. It is bragging on Jesus and what he has done for me and through me.

Unfortunately, I can't remember many of the interesting events of my life. Since I did not keep a journal, what is recorded here is from memory. Because I am ninety years old, I can't recall many things, and decades later some recollections are a bit fuzzy.

I wish I could mention more of the people who played a significant role in my life. The old saying "no man is an island" certainly holds true with me. I wouldn't be where I am without the help of many people, ranging from family to teachers to friends to fellow pastors to church members. The list goes on and on.

My three children encouraged me to write this book. During these years, I still enjoyed driving to places where they felt it was not safe for me to drive alone. They were fantastic in driving me. My wife, Montez was no longer interested or able to travel as much. As I took these long trips with Jim, Dianne, or Eric, I would share many of the things they had not heard before about my early life and spiritual journey. At first they thought I should write these things down; then they began to gently insist on it. Later others encouraged it as well, so I finally felt it would be a good idea. I started out by leaving notes that could be shared with a few people who might be interested. Then the project began to grow. Eventually, we decided it should be a book made available to everyone.

I am greatly indebted to Dianne. She encouraged me the most in this undertaking. She took on the monumental task of typing up the manuscript from my handwritten notes. Next we sent everything to Jim, who went through the drafts to edit and proofread them.

I have often said that of all the blessings God has given me the wonderful people he has brought into my life are the greatest. I wish I could name all of them, but there are too many.

Marrying into a family with a similar background turned out to be a great blessing. Montez's family were very, very good people. Her parents were as good to me as anyone could possibly ask. Her sister, Peggy, and her brother, Bill, were very kind. In our early marriage and parenting, her parents were very poor, but they still managed to help us. Now both her parents and both her siblings have passed on. My parents and six of my siblings have passed on as well.

It is my prayer and desire that when you read this book, if you have not already given your life to Jesus Christ, you will do so. It is wonderful.

Of all the amazing things that have happened in my life, Jesus coming into my heart was the *most amazing*! My marriage, my children, my career, and all the other things cannot compare to that wonderful day in the cotton field in the Mississippi delta.

1

EARLY YEARS AND EDUCATION

I WAS BORN IN ARIZONA BECAUSE PAPA WAS OUT THERE TO find work.

Between the late 1920s and early 1930s, we moved back and forth from Arkansas to Arizona twice. Leonard, the oldest child, was born in Arkansas before the family's first trip out west. On August 21, 1931, I was born in Glendale, and soon after that we headed back east.

It was during the Great Depression, but I don't think my birth was depressing to my parents; they probably were wondering just how they would get by. We were poorer than poor, and sometimes there was just no food. But somehow that didn't hold me back from being a fat baby.

I don't want to say I was a mama's boy, but if she put me down to take care of something else, I would get so mad I would headbutt the floor. Between being a chubby little baby and just preferring to have Mama carry me around everywhere, I didn't start walking until I was eighteen months old. That might have gone on even longer, but soon I wasn't the baby anymore. My brother Luther joined us in 1933.

One day the following year, we three brothers were at a neighbor's house, when our aunt came and got us. She told us that now we had a baby sister. Rosa was baby number four, and she sure was a tiny little thing.

That same year we moved back to Arizona. The trip has remained in my mind because as we were traveling out there our car broke down. We went the rest of the way on a train. When we finally arrived, we moved into a one-room, dirt-floor house—more like a shed, actually. We then moved to another house called the Ranch.

One day we were outside playing and chasing each other around the yard. We didn't pay much attention to the two men who drove up in a car and began to talk with Papa. He got into the car with the men and left. Playtime came to a screeching halt. We had no idea where they were taking Papa or why they were taking him.

The next day Mama loaded us four little ones into the car and headed to Phoenix.

Luther, Leonard, James, and Rosa.

As we were going down a mountain, we had a wreck. The car went out of control, did a flip, and then landed upright. It was a miracle that not only was no one killed but also no one was seriously injured. The only injuries were a bruised shoulder (me) and a knock on the head (Mama). I don't remember how we finally made it to Phoenix, but we got there.

The next day Mama took us to a big building. We walked down a hallway that didn't have any walls but had bars instead. We came to one place, where Papa was standing behind the bars. Later we learned he had been arrested for stealing a saddle from a cowboy! Mama basically begged the officials to let Papa out. After a stern talk about taking responsibility for the four little ones—and yes, another on the way—Papa was released from jail.

Shortly thereafter, Leland, the fourth boy, came to us. It was 1936, and we were still in the throes of the Depression.

Leonard started first grade, and I started kindergarten in Arizona. We were going to school one morning, and the crossing guard at Grande Avenue told us to wait until he took us across the street. One boy took off running across the street, ignoring the crossing guard. Leonard saw that and immediately did the same. I saw all of that and took off right after them. A car was coming down the street and somehow barely missed me. Lessons learned:

1. Always listen to the crossing guard.
2. Big brothers aren't always right.
3. God had his hand on us early on.

Soon we moved back to Arkansas, where Mama was from and where her family still lived, and in 1938 we welcomed son number five: Loland, also known as Tite. The second girl, Ruth, was born in 1940, then Ruby in 1941, Lewis in 1942, and Esther in 1944. We moved to Mississippi in 1945, and Ethel, the youngest, was born there in 1946. We had six boys and five girls.

Point of interest here: Up through Tite, *all* the children had blond hair and blue eyes and were very thin—all of them, that is, *but* me. I had black hair and green eyes and was what you might call *husky*! All the boys' names started with an *L*—except mine, which started with a *J*. I was just destined to be different from the rest of the pack! I was the second child of eleven, but I was as big as Leonard and much bigger than the younger ones.

My parents were intelligent, but they were not overly educated. Mama only made it to the eighth grade, and Papa only to the fourth grade. Papa was born in southwest Mississippi in April 1892, and Mama was born on March 10, 1906, in Ola, Arkansas. They were married in Heafer, Arkansas, in 1928.

Mama and Papa: Agnes and Bernard Fortinberry.

Education was never a priority for Papa. Discipline, however, was a high priority. My parents' methods of punishment were different. She believed in spanking; he believed in beating. The only scripture I ever remember him quoting us was "Spare the rod and spoil the child," and he didn't spare it. Papa was not a Christian at that time. Mama was a believer, but she was not able to go to church, since she always had two or three babies in diapers.

Back in Arkansas, Papa started farming. Our main crop was cotton; it was the cash crop for what little cash we had. Life was hard, but Papa was a very good farmer. Growing up on the farm was very tough. The days were long and started well before the sun rose. Our transportation was mules and a wagon. I was about nine years old when we got our first pickup. We were poor, as most people were back in those days, and grew nearly everything we ate. We had chickens for eggs and meat, hogs for meat and lard, and cows for milk, butter, and cream. We also had large gardens for fresh vegetables and for canning for winter. We had a cornfield that supplied us with fresh corn, canned corn, and hominy, and we had enough to take some to the grist mill to be ground up for meal. The man who ground the corn was paid with one-fourth of what he ground. We also had sorghum cane for syrup, which was a staple in those days. Most of what we bought was flour, sugar, and coffee.

Often there was not much meat on the table, but it would include rabbit, squirrel, and basically whatever else we could kill, skin, and eat. We ate a lot of vegetables. One time we didn't have any meat, just greens and beans. Mama always fixed them in big pots, and we would take our plates over and get our food straight from the pots. I didn't like greens. It didn't matter whether they were turnip greens, mustard greens, or collard greens—I just didn't like greens. I told Papa I didn't like them. He said he didn't care and that I was going to eat the greens. I decided to eat the greens first and get them out of the way so I could enjoy my beans. By the time I finished the greens, all the beans were gone. I cried!

We worked in the cotton fields starting at an early age. But with eleven of us, there was plenty of help. We would plow the fields, pick the cotton, and yes, even go to school—sometimes.

We usually moved about every two years. Our situation was not the same as the typical sharecropper. We would rent the farm but provided our own livestock and equipment. The rent payment was usually one-fourth or one-third of the money we made selling cotton. We would wait until the end of the season for our garden before we moved, plus Papa was also looking for the best deal on renting the next farm.

Our houses were usually very small. Four or five rooms—*rooms*, not bedrooms—was the usual size. Sometimes an enclosed back porch was one of the rooms. One can imagine thirteen people living in a four-room house. In the summer, we lived with a lot of "relative humidity."

a mule in different fields. It was "quittin' time." I had one row and a half to finish my field. Papa went on to the barn. My mule decided it was time for him to quit too. I decided to finish my field. My mule and I had quite a confrontation. I wouldn't quit, and he wouldn't go back to finish. We wound up plowing up lots of cotton. I got very angry and beat the mule. It did no good. I was so furious that if I'd had a gun I would have killed that mule.

That night as I was praying, God spoke to me.

"You got mad at the mule today, didn't you?"

"Yes, Lord!"

"You were angry enough to kill the mule?"

"Yes, Lord!"

"What are you going to do when a man makes you that angry?"

That night, after God had gently convicted me of my sin and forgiven me when I confessed, he took that anger away. I never got mad like that again.

We had neighbors down the road who we played with a lot. The Shearers had five boys: Leighton, Donald, Kenneth, Douglas, and Robert Bentley. They had a little cousin, Montez, who would come and visit often. During the summer she would stay a week or so. Mrs. Shearer—Aunt Beatrice—loved having her visit, since she had nothing but boys around. I really didn't pay much attention to Montez when she came to visit—that is, not until she was a little older.

During the eleventh grade, I missed more than half the school year but was able to pass. During my senior year, I got a job driving a school bus. I was allowed to go to school, provided I gave half my salary, twenty-five dollars per month, to Papa. Leonard left school in the tenth grade and joined the Army. Luther left too. Most of my brothers got their general equivalency diploma (GED), and some went on to college after serving in the military. Rosa stayed in school and finished, then went to college and got her master's degree. Ethel finished high school as well. All the other kids dropped out of school. Life was hard, and the general feeling was "anything out there is better than this." I was the only boy in my family to finish high school.

While it seems like I have said only negative things about Papa, he did a lot of good things for us. He taught us about honesty and a hard work ethic. Papa let us build a baseball field in the pasture for the community baseball team. When our team went to other communities, he took us all in the pickup. He would often take a load of us to a river, where we went skinny-dipping.

Just before graduation we had a party for our senior class. One of the boys in our class was sweet on our most popular girl. She did not feel the same way. One of our teachers was young and just out of college. He had his eye on this same girl, and she was attracted to him. After the party the teacher took her home. The boy became furious. He and this girl had never dated; he just liked her so much and felt the teacher shouldn't be seeing her. He wanted to go beat up the teacher but was afraid to try it by himself. He asked if someone would help him, and another boy said yes. I had no car, and this jealous boy was my ride.

He drove to a road the teacher would take back to school and pulled the car over to wait for him. I did not want to be a part of this. Not only did I not want to be in on it but I also could not let them do this either. While we sat on the side of the road, I prayed to God for guidance— an intervention or something. I was just so worried not only for the safety of the teacher but for us as well. I could not stand by and let two boys beat up the teacher. I would not help them, and I hated to go against my friends.

What could I do? Pray! Pray hard! Pray very hard!

We waited and waited and waited. The teacher never came back down that road; he took a different road back to school after taking her home. God intervened, and the big fight did not occur. Thank you, dear Lord.

My two honors as a senior were as follows: I was elected president of my senior class, and an award was given by the faculty to the best all-around student during the four years of high school. I was extremely proud of that award, considering how much school I had missed during those four years. Since I had a job during my senior year, I was able to play football, basketball, and baseball. I still had to work in the fields; I just didn't have to miss too much school to do it.

SENIOR YEAR—DUBLIN HIGH SCHOOL, 1950.

I wanted to go to college to be a football coach. I had no money, and my parents had no money, so I saw no way.

God intervened in the following manner: On a Boy Scouts retreat, I was asked by the leader, Melvin LaVail, if I would look after the younger boys while he took the older ones. While we were talking one night, he asked about my plans for the future. As we talked, he said he had a friend who had a business in which he hired boys to work and earn all college expenses. We went to meet him in Hattiesburg, at Mississippi Southern—now the University of Southern Mississippi. After our first interview, he offered me a job at the college canteen, which included everything from opening the store, to making coffee and food, to selling general merchandise. The week after I graduated from high school, I left for college with thirteen dollars in my pocket. As it turns out, the job turned into a full college scholarship, and I was allowed to work overtime to earn spending money.

During my years at Southern, there were not many honors. There were some things that were significant about that time though. The draft was active for the Korean War. God miraculously prevented me from being conscripted; he had something else planned for me.

The next thing that happened was God had called me to preach. For years my heart had been set on going to college in order to become a high school football coach and to have the kind of positive influence on my players that my coach had had on me. I wanted to be a football coach, not a preacher, but I knew I wanted to be in God's will. To be in God's will, though, I had to change my major from physical education to speech—another significant event. I was elected president of the Baptist Student Union (BSU) during my junior year. I also was ordained on April 12, 1952, and called to pastor two churches: Cagle's Crossing and Locke Station.

Then there was that little cousin of my neighbors' whom

I never really noticed. Well, when she was seventeen, I noticed her. Man, did I notice her! She was a real beauty, and later that summer we started dating.

MRS. MONTEZ FORTINBERRY, NÉE SHEARER.

Montez Shearer and I were married on December 28, 1952. She was still in high school, and I was in college. We could not afford to get married, but here was how it happened: Floyd Higginbotham, my lifelong friend, was from the same church and community. Like me, he was called to preach, and we had agreed that when we each got married I would do his wedding, and he would do mine—for free! We did not announce our wedding. We told our family and a few friends. Montez's parents; her sister, Peggy; her brother, Bill; and her aunt and uncle, the ones she visited every summer, were in attendance. On Sunday night, right after church, Montez came to the front of the church, then Floyd came up front and married us. Total cost of the wedding: three dollars for the license. We've been together sixty-nine years. We got our money's worth! Floyd and Effie got married in South Carolina while he was in the Army. They have been married for over sixty-five years. I still owe him a wedding.

Montez finished high school in 1953. I came home from Hattiesburg on weekends to preach. We lived with her parents for several months, until she finished high school. During that time she gave her life to Christ, and I baptized her and several others.

During the summer I worked and pastored my churches: Cagle's Crossing and Locke Station. That fall we moved to Hattiesburg while I finished college, still pastoring my churches. As I finished school in April 1954, our first child, Jim, was born at the Hattiesburg Methodist Hospital. We had no money and no insurance. The doctor who delivered him didn't charge me anything, and the hospital let me pay monthly.

After graduating I needed to go on to seminary because I had no theology credits. My student minister at Southern Miss had counseled me in many ways while I was in Hattiesburg. He was a great help in getting me accepted at New Orleans Baptist Seminary.

In the fall of 1954, we moved to New Orleans for seminary. I was still pastoring two churches. Cagle's Crossing, near Tutwiler, Mississippi, was 370 miles from New Orleans; and Leaf Church, in McClain, Mississippi, was 175 miles away. I alternated between the two every other weekend.

When I first went to New Orleans, I left the car for Montez and took a train down there, arriving with a whopping fourteen-dollar bankroll. My cousin had written and invited me to stay with them until we got settled. The problem was, when I got to New Orleans, they were away on vacation. I found a hotel and checked in without asking the price. The next day I found out it was seven dollars— half my entire bankroll. Now I had seven dollars, no job, and no place to stay, in a strange city.

I immediately started looking for work and got a job at Western Auto that afternoon, scheduled to start the next day. I ate very little and stayed at the YMCA that night. Soon I was down to three dollars. I asked for an advance on my pay, but the company didn't provide it. Another salesman loaned me five dollars until payday.

I spent the night at the bus station. During the night policemen would go through the terminal to clear out the homeless people sleeping there. They would walk up to them and ask for their ticket and where they were going. If they couldn't produce a ticket, they would make them move out and warn them not to come back. I was sitting there in a nice white shirt, Bible in hand, and my suitcase next to me. It appeared I was going somewhere, and I didn't dare fall asleep. The next morning I went straight to work at Western Auto.

When I got off work that evening, I still had no idea where I would spend the night. I had no more money for a room and no place to stay. If I went back to the bus station, I could be arrested. Also, I couldn't miss another night's sleep. I started walking down the sidewalk, looking for a park—more specifically, a park bench. Once again, God provided for my needs. As I passed a hot tamale stand, my assistant manager at the store just happened to stop by there to get takeout for his wife and children. He saw me and invited me to spend the night with his family.

On my fourth day in New Orleans, my meals consisted of one twelve-cent hamburger for breakfast, another one for lunch, and a third one for supper. On day five it was a five-cent Snickers bar for breakfast, another one for lunch, and a final one for supper.

I worked until Saturday evening, then caught a bus to Hattiesburg, where I had another cousin, and spent the night there. Then I borrowed a neighbor's car and went to preach at my 175-miles-away church. They paid me twenty dollars there, then I drove back to my cousin's and returned the car, then caught a bus back to New Orleans and got paid thirty dollars for my first week's work. *That* was my first week in New Orleans to get my seminary training.

The seminary years were hard for both Montez and me. I had a full course load at school, worked a job for thirty-six hours per week, and pastored my two churches. When we went to the 370-miles-away church, I would get off work at eight on Saturday evenings. Montez would have the car packed and ready to go. I would drive all night to get there. After church on Sunday, I would rest two or three hours, drive back to New Orleans on Sunday night, then go to work on Monday morning.

On Wednesday nights I attended a church near our apartment. One night I decided to go out with the church on visitation. I was nervous, but they assured us that we would be paired with someone with experience. We got our assignments, and they paired me with a little old lady. I was supposed to be the experienced team member.

While we were out, we walked down a street to an assignment. Most people didn't have air-conditioning, so they sat outside. We saw and heard a big commotion ahead of us. A three-foot chain-link fence was between the sidewalk and the yard. As we got closer to the commotion, it appeared to be a family feud. I wanted to avoid getting any closer to it. A man had a metal chair, and he was swinging it and chasing away others. Now we were right there and couldn't walk away, so I approached the man face-to-face. He stopped swinging the chair and looked at me. I said, "How are you doing?"

He said, "Fine, how are you doing?"

I lied and said, "Fine." Truth was, I was scared to death.

I told him we were out visiting for our church and would like to come in and visit. He said, "Come on in." We went into the yard and had a good visit and invited them to church.

❧

While we were in New Orleans, on December 26, 1956, Dianne was born. We had insurance to cover this because the seminary required it. After she was born, Montez's mother came to New Orleans to help us.

Money was scarce, and food was not always easy to get. When I went to the churches to preach, they would feed us lunch after the Sunday service, then usually give us something to take home—loaves of bread, jars of food, things along that line.

One Sunday a lady served venison for lunch. I had not eaten any before and did not like it all. Guess what? She gave me a large package of it to take home. When I was nearly home, driving over Lake Pontchartrain, I came very close to throwing the package into the lake to feed the alligators. I took it home to throw it away. When I told Montez's mom what had happened, she said, "Let me try cooking it." She made it, and it was delicious!

"O ye of little faith!"

2

VOCATION

As I was growing up on the farm, I knew that when I grew up I did not want to be a farmer. That was about all I knew. I had helped some with building but was not a carpenter. When I accepted Christ, I knew I wanted to serve God. After finishing my last season of football, I saw how much influence our coach had on all the boys. I decided I wanted to be a football coach. There was no way for that to happen, though, because there was no money for college. I was offered a half scholarship but couldn't get the rest of the money.

As I noted above, God intervened at a Boy Scout retreat, and I was able to secure a job in Hattiesburg. This enabled me to pursue my college education at Southern Miss.

My major in college was physical education so I could

prepare to coach. One course involved actually coaching a grammar school football team, the equivalent of peewee football today. We played the other schools in Hattiesburg. We had a fair team and won about half our games.

During my second year of college, my boss said he wanted me to work for him when I finished school. He would guarantee me more money than I could ever make coaching and teaching school. I began taking some courses in business. My boss operated the Wimpy's on Southern's campus. It was basically a general store for college kids, where one could buy school supplies as well as coffee, food, and even underwear—truly a "general" store.

At one point it looked as though he might lose the contract on the campus Wimpy's. He wanted me to continue to work with him and asked me if I would go to Brandon, where he had a small store and an auto garage. I worked at this business and attended Mississippi College, a Baptist school located several miles away. I accepted the job and went to Brandon. He provided me a two-seat Model A car to drive back and forth. During that term at Mississippi College, as related elsewhere, God called me to preach. That fall my boss got a new contract back in Hattiesburg, and I went back to Southern and completed my bachelor's degree.

After that summer at Mississippi College, I went home for a few days. I told my family I was going to be a preacher. Mama was overjoyed with the news, and the rest were okay with it.

Mama was attending a little Nazarene church near their home. She could walk to church. She told the pastor about me, and he told her the next time I was home I could preach there.

The time came for me to preach my first sermon. I had prepared for weeks, had my notes laid out in a notebook, and was extremely nervous. As I started, the notebook was opened at the right page. When I read my scripture, I inadvertently closed the notebook. I was too nervous to go back and try to find the right spot. I went the rest of the way without my notes. Somehow, by God's grace, I got through it.

My second sermon was different. A group of us from the BSU had a prison ministry in the city jail. On one of our visits, policemen were dragging in a very uncooperative inmate. This was a major disturbance to our work. To make matters worse, the guy who was going to preach didn't show up.

We got through the singing okay. Then the other team members looked at me and said, "James, you're a preacher. You have to preach." So I delivered my second sermon in a jailhouse, with no preparation.

In those days, it was customary to ordain a preacher only after they were a pastor, or while they were being considered for one. My friend Jerry Rogers, who had also been called to preach, suggested we ask for ordination. This was in April 1952, and neither of us had a church where we were actively preaching at the time. An ordination council was called together at our church, First Baptist Church of Hattiesburg. Neither of us were really qualified, but somehow we were approved.

One interesting part of this ordination was when I was asked to explain my position on the doctrines of the Rapture of the Church and the Millennium. I knew nothing but gave an answer anyway. It was not a good answer, but the council members didn't agree with each other, so they started debating among themselves, which let me off the hook.

Locke Station Baptist Church

In June 1952, I was called to Locke Station Baptist Church, near my parents' place. I was home for the summer recuperating from an appendectomy. Mama had recently started going to this church.

The call to go to Locke Station was very strange. One Saturday I visited a man in his store. He was a deacon at the church and told me that their pastor had just left, and they were looking for a new one. He asked if I would preach the next day, and I agreed to do so.

On Sunday morning, when Sunday school was over, the deacon in charge, said, "Well, it don't look like we have a preacher, so we will go home." The deacon who had invited me to preach was away that day. I stood up and told them what had happened the day before and that I had come to preach. He said, "Fine, come on."

I preached my sermon and spoke a little about myself and my plans. When I finished, I said, "I understand you are looking for a pastor. Well, I'm available."

They looked at each other. Nobody said anything. Then I said, "I understand that Baptists vote on calling a pastor." Still no one said anything. I went on, "If you would like to have me as your pastor, raise your hand." Most people raised their hands. I didn't ask if there were any nays.

So there, in an illegal business meeting, led and chaired by a stranger, I was called to my first church. Now, to soften the blow a little, understand that this was only for the two months of the summer, and it was only for every other Sunday. I would go back to school in the fall.

When the summer had ended, they had done nothing about calling a pastor. One Sunday I said, "Next time is my last Sunday. You need to get someone."

The man who had first invited me spoke up and said, "We have our pastor. We don't need to look anywhere." They voted for me to stay. At that time I didn't own a car. I walked up and down the rural roads to do my visiting. When I would go to Cagle's Crossing every other Sunday, fifty miles away, I would hitchhike. Sometimes it would be in a truck, sometimes in a car, but fortunately never a horse-drawn wagon. Occasionally, my dad let me take his pickup truck. At the end of that summer, as I headed back to school in Hattiesburg, the church raised enough money to make a down payment on a car, a 1950 Chevrolet, for me to drive back and forth. The trip one way was over two hundred miles. Needless to say, we needed a car.

OUR FIRST CAR, A 1950 CHEVROLET.

God blessed us that summer. The church grew, and I baptized several people, mostly adults. One woman I baptized in the creek was very heavy. She was not only very heavy but she was also very scared, and *I* was very nervous. When I started putting her underwater, she started backing up several steps. I had to chase her down the creek, but it was finally successful.

Once I was back at Southern, I had to set a schedule to cover both churches on the same weekend. To accommodate them both, I would go to one church on Saturday night and then back on Sunday night; then I would go to the other church on Sunday morning and Sunday afternoon. This only lasted for two weekends, though, because that was how long we—as in the churches and I—took to realize that would not work. After that we went back to the regular schedule of alternating weekends between the churches.

I stayed another year at Locke Station after the "legitimate call" in August.

Cagle's Crossing

UNION CHAPEL WAS THE ACTUAL NAME OF THE CHURCH,
BUT EVERYONE CALLED IT CAGLE'S CROSSING.

Cagle's Crossing was my home church—where I grew up, where I was saved, and where later Montez and I were married. The church had invited me to preach a youth revival in August 1952. Just after I had been called to Locke Station, a deacon from Cagle's Crossing called to tell me they were looking for a pastor. I said, "What a coincidence. I'm looking for a church." This, too, was a part-time church, meeting on different Sundays than Locke Station. They called me as pastor. God blessed our work there through the summer, with several people being saved and baptized.

ROUNDAWAY LAKE IN THE HEART OF THE MISSISSIPPI DELTA.

When fall came, the people of Cagle's Crossing, along with the people of Locke Station, collected enough money, above and beyond their tithe, to make a down payment on the car. I stayed at Cagle's Crossing for another year. When I resigned and went back to school, I had the unusual experience of coming back after several weeks—a story related in more detail elsewhere in this book.

Several things occurred during my second stint as pastor at my home church that still stand out in my memory. The first funeral I conducted was for a stillborn baby, which was very sad, even in the context of funerals. The second funeral I conducted was especially tragic. A family—father, mother, son—were in a small boat fishing on a lake. The son was seventeen years old. I knew him from school. While they were fishing, a group in a speedboat ran over their small boat. The three occupants were scattered but uninjured. The father could swim; the mother could not. The son was a good swimmer. The mother was drowning, and the son swam over to rescue her. He was able to save her, but he drowned in the effort. That was extremely sad and difficult for me as an inexperienced young preacher.

Among those who were saved at Cagle's Crossing was Paul Broadway, whom I had known since I was fourteen years old. One Wednesday night Paul and Jean were in church with their two-and-a-half-year-old son, Terry. Everything seemed fine then. The next morning I was up early tending to Jim, who was now four months old. I heard a car horn coming down the road. I saw that it was Paul. I waved, and when I did he stopped and came running up to my door, yelling, "Come with me. My baby is dying!"

I quickly dressed and went with him. I insisted on driving because he was too distraught. I drove one hundred miles per hour and got to a doctor's home. We woke up the doctor. He examined Terry and pronounced him dead. Paul nearly died from sorrow, but soon gave his life to Christ. Then he began to heal emotionally. After I left the church, he was called into the ministry. He was one of the most avid soul winners I ever knew. He wanted to tell others about Jesus. He never received a formal ministerial education, but even so he was an effective pastor.

This church building was only one room. We added two rooms while we were there—a major building project! Cagle's Crossing was both Baptist and Methodist in the same building, yet I was pastor to the entire congregation. The Methodist pastor only came once a month. We were there just over three years altogether.

The salary was 90 percent of their offering. Usually this was about eighteen to twenty dollars per week for the entire three years. During this time we had moved to New Orleans, so every other weekend we were driving 740 miles round trip for twenty dollars a week and God's glory!

Leaf Church

SINCE LEAF CHURCH SERVED BOTH BAPTISTS AND
METHODISTS, IT WAS SIMPLY CALLED LEAF CHURCH.

After we left Locke Station, I still went back to Cagle's Crossing every other week. A church about 70 miles from Hattiesburg asked me to come preach in view of a call. Locke Station and Cagle's Crossing were 240 miles from school, so a church 70 miles away seemed like it was right down the street. Their search process was to hear several preachers, then vote on which one they wanted. We got the largest number of votes, thus went our call to Leaf. It was another part-time arrangement, both Baptist and Methodist, so now I was pastor of two Baptist-Methodist churches at once.

Our time here was not marked by any standout events, but the pastorate provided me with further pastoral experience and opportunities to preach. When we moved from Hattiesburg to New Orleans, the church was now about 175 miles away from where we lived, so they gave me a raise from twenty dollars to thirty dollars a week.

While pastoring at Leaf, I continued to work at Western Auto. When finances were low, God came through by helping me have a good sales week.

We had fewer converts here. I had been accustomed to having many more; otherwise, things went well.

Pine Level Baptist Church

After we left Cagle's Crossing, the Pine Level Baptist Church called us. This church was near Leaf. Some members had relatives in the other church. This was as I was nearing finishing seminary.

We were there ten months. It was the first time I did not have one convert. In some ways, however, our connection to this church was different. Every five years they had a homecoming revival. This was a major event. For fifteen years they had me come and preach that revival.

3

WALNUT GROVE YEARS

WALNUT GROVE BAPTIST CHURCH.

As I was nearing graduation from seminary, I began praying for a full-time church. In the spring of 1958, just before finishing seminary, we were called to our first full-time church, Walnut Grove Baptist Church, in Mississippi. I commuted back and forth to New Orleans for four months, until I graduated.

Walnut Grove Baptist Church, in Walnut Grove, Mississippi, was known for bringing in new seminary graduates to pastor for a few years. My name, among several others, was given to them.

One day the man who had submitted my name told me their pulpit committee was coming to hear me preach on a given Sunday. I prepared my very best "sugar stick"—an expression for a best sermon possible. I was on cloud nine, anticipating their coming. Sunday came, but the committee didn't, so now I was deflated and disappointed. That night I went to church in a low mood, bringing a "just-get-by" sermon, nothing special. Guess what? The committee showed up to hear me. I did the best I could with what I had to offer. After that less-than-my-best sermon, they still wanted to talk with me. We talked a long while, then I had to drive 175 miles back to New Orleans. They invited us to go to Walnut Grove for a trial sermon. When the church voted, it was a unanimous vote.

About three weeks later, on seminary campus, I overheard some students talking about what they were reading in a newspaper. One of them said, "I guess that is God's punishment on Walnut Grove because they didn't call me as pastor." That got my attention. I approached the group of guys and asked what they were talking about. They showed me the newspaper. There was a story that Walnut

Grove had been torn up by a tornado. I told them I had just been called there and would start in three weeks. The man who had commented on it being God's punishment later came and apologized. This all happened in March 1958. Our organist at the church was killed during the storm. Another church member died a few days later. One lady was sitting on her couch, watching the news about the storm. The storm hit immediately, and she was carried up into a tree while still sitting on the couch. Rescuers had to get her and the couch down from the tree. She was not hurt.

We moved around the first of April, even though I was not finishing school until July. Montez and the children stayed in Walnut Grove while I went back to school from Tuesday through Friday. I carpooled with some other guys the 250 miles each way.

Walnut Grove was a small town of roughly five hundred people, off Highway 35, about halfway between Carthage and Forest. There were three small churches: a Methodist, a Presbyterian, and the Baptist. The local school housed all twelve grades on one campus.

Unique to Walnut Grove, in lieu of a town square, they had a town *triangle*. The bank, the barbershop, the grocery store, the five-and-dime, and other shops were all laid out around the triangle.

The church was a classic red brick structure, and the

parsonage across the street was built from matching red brick, with a green shingle roof. Ms. Fanny Upton, the church pianist, lived across the street from us. About once or twice a year I would get a call from this sweet elderly lady that a snake was in her house, and I'd go over and kill it or get it out of the house.

During our first year in Walnut Grove, we learned that Mama had developed breast cancer when she was fifty-two years old. She didn't go to a doctor; there was no money and no insurance. When the cancer was discovered, she had a mastectomy in August 1958, but it was too late, and she died the following January. Grandpa, her papa, paid all the bills. My youngest brother, Lewis, and the four youngest girls were still living at home then.

When Mama died, Papa was still not saved. All along he would not allow me to talk to him about being saved. Not long after Mama died, though, he did accept Christ. One day I was in my office in Walnut Grove. I had a special burden to pray for him for about an hour. A few days later, he called me about another matter. Then he said, "I have joined the church." Back then "joining the church" meant "I got saved."

Later, when I was visiting him, he told me how it happened. He had come in the house after being out somewhere. He was eating alone and became so burdened that he prayed to be saved. He was! The time he was saved was the same hour of the same day I was in my office praying for him—130 miles away.

He started going to four churches in the community every week: the Baptist, Nazarene, Church of God, and a Pentecostal. He was sixty-six at that time, fourteen years older than Mama.

Three years later Papa died of a stroke. Again, there was no money and no insurance. Rosa's husband, Glen, paid that bill for the doctor and hospital.

The salary at Walnut Grove was $3,600 per year. The church provided us a house (parsonage), but I paid the utilities. There was no travel allowance or insurance. The only way we could get by financially was that I preached three or four revivals each year, which usually brought in $100 for each one.

Even though our church income grew by 50 percent the first year, we didn't receive a raise. After a steady raise in income, we received $600 a year for travel expenses. When Eric was born, during a snowstorm in January 1962, there was no money and no insurance. The doctor didn't charge anything, and I made monthly payments on the hospital bill, which several people from the church contributed to in order to help us. We never got a raise in salary during that four-year ministry.

The parsonage was a small three-bedroom house. When we had revivals, the evangelist would stay at our house, which was difficult since the house only had one bathroom.

I made lots of mistakes there. I often look back and wonder why they didn't fire me. But they knew I loved God, and I loved them.

We were also fortunate enough to have people at the church who took my young family under their wing, prayed for us, guided us, and watched out for us and our little ones. One couple in particular, Junior and Frances Rogers, became as close as family.

They owned a business just outside town, where he had a furniture and appliance warehouse, and she ran a beauty shop in the south end of the building. Once or twice a month, Montez and I would go over one evening to relax, play Scrabble, and eat popcorn and peanut brittle. They turned out to be lifelong friends, and we are forever grateful for them. Even after their passing, their children—Susan and Dale—are still very close to us.

JAMES AND JUNIOR AND FRANCES ROGERS.
THE GAME OF SCRABBLE WAS SERIOUS BUSINESS.

Before going to Walnut Grove, I had never been to a deacons' meeting or to a committee meeting—all that was new to me. One of our men nominated me to be the Royal Ambassadors (RA) director for the association. I had never even heard of the RAs, a boys' mission program. I was elected even though I was not at the meeting.

I was RA leader for our boys at church. We had a good ministry because I had to study and learn it from scratch. We had weekly meetings and often went on camping trips. I had the privilege of leading some of the boys to accept Christ.

We also started a baseball team. It was mostly boys from our church, but we had players from other churches. The team became very good and played in a league in Carthage, a larger town ten miles north of us. We usually won all our games, so finally Carthage would not allow us to play in their league, because they didn't want us beating their teams.

Now, after nearly sixty years have gone by, it seems that our most lasting work there was with those boys. They became leaders in their churches and communities. Ray Britt became a bank president. Haywood Reeves became a high school principal. Dale Rogers became a successful businessman, then later in life had a second career as a pastor. I had the opportunity to visit with them and their wives in October 2019. That evening of fellowship with them, fifty-seven years after we moved from Walnut Grove, was a tremendous blessing.

Our "youth group" from Walnut Grove.

4

TURKEY CREEK YEARS

TURKEY CREEK FIRST BAPTIST.

ONE SATURDAY AFTERNOON I WAS WASHING MY CAR IN OUR driveway in Walnut Grove. A car pulled into the driveway, and four men got out. They identified themselves as C. T. Lewis, Sonny Jones, Elmer Owens, and Leonard Helms, a pulpit committee from Florida. We visited most of the afternoon. As we were wrapping up the visit, they invited us to go to Florida for a trial sermon at Turkey Creek First Baptist Church. This invitation came before they heard me preach. They spent that night in a nearby town and came to church to hear me the next day. At that time we had teenage boys as ushers and greeters. When those four men came up the steps, one of the boys said, "If you are who we think you are, you are not welcome here."

The Lord had already spoken to me, so in my mind our trip down in view of a call was not necessary—I already knew. The people down there did need to meet us though. It was a good weekend, and the vote to call us was unanimous. This all happened rather quickly, considering we weren't in trouble or being chased off. The pulpit committee came in the first week of August 1962. We went for our trial sermon the very next week, then moved down there around the end of August to ensure that Jim and Dianne would start school on time in September.

Turkey Creek was a rural community about twenty miles east of Tampa, Florida. This was in a time before the Bucs, Rays, Lightning, Disney World, and Universal Studios, so church and school activities were strongly supported by the people in the area. The white stucco building housed one of the largest rural churches in the state and was located a short distance from Turkey Creek High School. Most of the young people in the church attended school there, and several of the faculty attended our church faithfully each Sunday. John Yost, the minister of music at the church, was also the chorus teacher at the high school. His wife, Velma, taught second grade at the elementary school. The high school boasted one of the top agricultural programs in the state, and its sports teams— and their rivalries—were focal points for the community. Several of the families in the church were farmers, whose livelihood was cattle, peanuts, or the big crops in that area, strawberries and oranges.

As we pulled into the carport, two little girls, Amanda and Melissa, came running up to greet us. They were staying with Doris Parrish, who lived very close to the church, while their parents were working. The girls' parents, Tom and Jewel MacPherson, both worked in the school system and were extremely active in our church. Unfortunately for us, they moved to Tennessee just two years after we arrived.

The Parrish family, Grady and Doris, and their six children, had been members for years. They served the church faithfully throughout my pastorate there and on after I left. Doris had grown up in the church, and her dad, Jim Goff, still attended. Her brother, Frank Goff, along with his entire family, were core faithful church members. When I began my ministry at Turkey Creek, Jim Goff was on up in years, but even though he was getting older he was faithful to attend every Sunday. Through this family the church was supplied with Sunday School and Training

Union teachers, choir members, deacons, bus ministry, committee members, nursery workers, and Vacation Bible School volunteers.

The explosion came at our very first business meeting.

It turned out that among some of my predecessors there had been some instances of issues of a personal nature, situations which I will not go into here.

At the business meeting, the church had received a request for the letters of recommendation for membership for the family to join a church in Kentucky. The fireworks came over whether to grant their letters. Some said yes; others said no. A compromise was reached by granting letters for the family, but not for the pastor. He didn't get his letter but was officially voted out of the church. Trying to moderate that first business meeting was one of my worst nightmares.

Deacons' meetings and business meetings were usually difficult. The deacons had two ironclad rules: "No business could come before the church unless it had been approved by the deacons first"; and "Nothing could come to the church unless it had been approved unanimously by all the deacons."

When we went to Turkey Creek, I had a feeling we would be there for ten years. One man in the community said, "You won't last two years." The church had many difficulties and I had to walk on eggshells for the first few years. Their experiences with their former pastors caused the people to be skeptical. One deacon promised me, "If you can stay here five years, we will put air-conditioning in the parsonage."

I did, and they did.

A few months after we had settled into the house, we ordered new furniture—from our good friends, the Rogers, back in Walnut Grove. They delivered the order personally and stayed on to visit with us a few days. Over the years they frequently came down to visit with us, and their home was always open to us when we went back up through Mississippi.

JUNIOR, FRANCES, MONTEZ, AND JAMES.

Despite some of the "personality challenges" at the church, God blessed us in wonderful ways. I got to perform a lot of weddings over the years there. Those young couples began their own families, and each year the church was blessed with the arrival of new babies. Montez began working in the nursery with Mrs. Mattie Mabry, and in a short amount of time they developed a superb nursery ministry. The church had a great place for all the little ones who were coming along.

We averaged baptizing fifty people per year while we were there. The church grew, Sunday School attendance increased, and participation in scheduled church activities was encouraging.

The church was a member of the Shiloh Baptist Association, which covered East Hillsborough County. During this period so many of the churches were led by outstanding pastors that it seemed like revivals were constantly in progress. First Baptist Church of Dover, the largest rural church in the state, was led by L. D. Gorley, a superb preacher and leader. Plant City First was pastored by Dr. Richard Bills, a wonderful pastor and gracious friend in the Lord. The outstanding evangelist James Smith, maybe the best pure preacher in the area, pastored several churches in the association over the years. Wayne Johnson, out at Youmans, was another outstanding preacher. Bob Coram, out at Valrico First Baptist; Wallace Register of Hopewell; Floyd Yarbrough, initially at Knights Baptist, then later at Berea Baptist; Alan Coryell; Truett Smith; and Al Livingston, pastor at Lebanon—all wonderful men and excellent pastors, many of them good friends as well. Often we preached revivals in each other's churches or invited each other to preach at homecomings, and we enjoyed prayer and fellowship at associational pastors' meetings.

Some of the revivals God blessed us with during the years at Turkey Creek are also worth revisiting. Our church secretary, Sarah Ford, had a cousin who was on the roster of the Boston Patriots—later renamed to the New England Patriots. Tony Romeo was a member of the Fellowship of Christian Athletes and a licensed minister. We contacted Tony, and he agreed to spend a week with us and bring in some of his associates from the FCA.

On the weekend before our revival began, the FCA held a big rally at the University of Tampa, where several professional athletes shared their testimony, signed autographs, and talked with the men and boys who gathered to hear them that day. The highlight of the event was an appearance by Paul Anderson, 1956 Olympic gold medalist in weightlifting, who was billed as "the world's strongest man." He gave a strength demonstration and shared highlights from his life's story leading up to the Olympics, giving all the glory to the Lord Jesus Christ.

The next Monday night he preached to a full house at our church. On Tuesday night Dave Wickersham and Don Demeter, starting pitcher and shortstop of the Detroit

Tigers, were preaching. The rest of the week either Tony would preach or have another Christian athlete in the pulpit. A regret from that week is that more people did not come to Christ, but it was a memorable time due to the Christian athletes who came and preached to us and the large crowds who came to hear them.

The year after that Adrian Rogers spent a week in revival with us. He and I had attended seminary in New Orleans at the same time. He was pastor at Merritt Island at the time, a couple of hours away on the East Coast, and it was wonderful to have him come over and preach for us.

Other excellent revivals took place during the meetings, led by some of my fellow pastors in the association: James Smith, L. D. Gorley, and Floyd Yarbrough, to name a few. We also had excellent meetings with Billy Barber, pastor of the First Baptist Church of Tampa, and Babb Adams from Temple Terrace. We had an excellent youth revival, with Jackie Hayes preaching and Terry Veazy leading the music.

One other highlight: In 1967 the Southern Baptist evangelist Dr. E. J. Daniels scheduled a tent revival on the fairgrounds of the Strawberry Festival in Plant City. The churches all worked together on the details and preparation required for a campaign of this magnitude. The meetings were well attended, and many decisions for Christ were made.

That same year we took our youth choir, led by Jim Studstill, down to Miami, where they joined with other youth choirs from across the state for a great program highlighted by special music from Anita Bryant.

When we first moved down there, the church had a fast-pitch softball team. After our pitcher, Alton Ford, moved to Lake City, we switched over to a slow-pitch league. The team was decent enough in the beginning. But as more of the boys who had come through the high school teams—coached by Jim Reed, Dan McMullen, and Wallace Brown—graduated and gravitated to our softball team, it developed into a championship team, and in the 1970s they were one of the top five church teams in the United States. In 1970 we started a women's slow-pitch softball team, and I was the coach that first year. In just a few weeks, the ladies jelled as a team and became tops in their league. In 1972 the church started a second men's team just to give some of the guys a chance to play who couldn't play at the level of the A team. Within a few years, they became good enough to win the local league on a regular basis.

During our second year at Turkey Creek, I became seriously ill from a complication of three problems and was hospitalized for eight days.

During that time I had a unique experience. I saw in a vision, or a dream, that I was moving down a country road. I could see in front of me an opening over the road

I was traveling, but I could not see beyond the door. The distance to the door was exactly three days. I understood this to mean I would pass through it in three days. To me, that door was death, but I was not afraid. I was concerned about my young family and asked God, "What about my family? What will they do?"

The answer came back. "That is not your family. It is my family. Don't worry about it."

Then I was concerned about the church. Things were settling down, and God was blessing us. I prayed, "Lord, what will happen to my church?"

The answer came again. "That is not your church. It is my church. Don't worry about it."

From that time on, for the next day or two, I was not worried about anything. Even though I could not see beyond the door, I knew my Savior was waiting to take me into his arms. I was excited and anxious about meeting him. I wanted to go on to him.

On Wednesday night, at about eight o'clock, the entire vision vanished. I never saw it again. Now remember Wednesday night was when churches do most of their praying for the sick. By this time several churches knew of my condition and were praying for me. I was back in the pulpit in a couple of weeks, although it took a few months to get back to full strength.

We had an active Royal Ambassador group at Turkey Creek like we had at Walnut Grove. One day a couple of us took the RAs to a popular summer spot, Lithia Springs. Lithia was a spring-fed body of water. Its large horseshoe-shaped swimming area was known for its cold, clear water and white sandy bottom, and this fed into the Alafia River that ran along its south side. It also had a beach area, pavilion-covered picnic tables, and a camping area.

One of the boys in our group was from a family who did not attend church. His mother was reluctant to allow him to go because he could not swim. I assured her that I would take care of him.

When we arrived at the springs, the boys were anxious to get in the water. We all had our swimsuits on underneath our clothing. The kids stripped down to their swimsuits instantly and were in the water prior to me even getting ready.

I was still near the car, when I heard a lot of noise and commotion from the water. I rushed down there and found the boy who could not swim was in the water and was in trouble, so I went straight in to help him. Just as I got in, another boy, who was overweight and not a very good swimmer, jumped on my back. This caught me completely off guard, and I was easily taken underwater. I was not a strong swimmer, so now there were three of us struggling in the water. We were underwater and couldn't see anything. I was holding the boy who couldn't swim, trying to get him to safety, but the other boy was on my shoulders. We were in serious trouble.

I heard all the other boys shouting, and that helped me to know which direction to go. I managed to get close enough that those on the bank took hold of the one boy who couldn't swim and pulled him to safety. The other boy, who was on my shoulders, was holding on tight, but I was able to get both of us out.

This was a harrowing experience, but it all turned out well. But that night I couldn't sleep, because I could only see us nearly drowning every time I closed my eyes. This went on for several nights. I thought it might be time for me to see a counselor.

I prayed fervently and felt a strange leading: I knew I had to go back to Lithia Springs to get a victory over this trauma. I had to go alone. I had to overcome those fears.

I went back to Lithia by myself and stood on the bank near where the incident occurred. I had to conquer it. I jumped in there and began to swim around, then dove down to where the springs fed the water. After a good bit of time in the water that afternoon, I went back home. From that day on, I never had another nightmare about any of it, because God took that from me.

Due to increasing attendance, we found ourselves running out of space after a couple of years. In 1965 we built two new buildings for educational space. Attendance continued to go up, so in 1968 we were led of the Lord to start a mission about seven miles south of the church that would serve the Durant community. One of our members, Charles Studstill, a former military chaplain, served as its first pastor, and several our key families were the charter members. After Charles moved on to another ministry, Bill Slate, also a member of Turkey Creek and whom I had the privilege of ordaining to the ministry, served as pastor of the mission church. Pleasant Grove Baptist Church—now Durant Baptist Church—is still active today over fifty years later.

PLEASANT GROVE BAPTIST CHURCH.

TENT REVIVAL.

One of the interesting things at Turkey Creek occurred when a man was saved who had an artificial leg made of cork. I told him he would need to remove that cork leg when he was baptized. He said, "No, I'll be fine," insisting he would be okay because he could walk around in his stock pond with no trouble.

We stepped down into the baptismal waters with no problems. He looked at me and grinned, as if to say, "I *told* you so." When I leaned him back in the water, he had no control over that leg. It went flying up out of the baptismal pool and splashed water almost to the ceiling. I was trying to hold him up, and that cork leg was floating on top of the water at nearly shoulder height. I finally managed to get his leg down under him. I looked at him and grinned, as if to say, "I told *you* so."

Another delightful thing happened that was unusual. I was invited to go with a group to the Holy Land. The church paid for me to go. It was a wonderful experience— truly a trip of a lifetime.

While I was on the tour, WPLA, the local radio station in Plant City, was doing a promotion at that time, and the promotion was that whoever was on vacation farthest from Plant City would win a three-day vacation stay in a nice hotel. To prove where the contestants were, the station must receive a postcard postmarked from that location. I sent a postcard from Israel. That was the farthest from Plant City, so I won a three-day free trip to Fort Lauderdale in a nice hotel. We enjoyed that time with the family, and it was in a place nicer than we had ever been before.

Once Eric started first grade, Montez began working at the elementary school as a teacher's aide. After a brief tenure as an aide, she began to get requests to help out as a substitute teacher. One of the neighboring schools, Pinecrest, brought her in for their sixth-grade class, and she taught there for a year and a half. They would have kept her on longer, and she would have stayed longer, but school system rules prohibited her being allowed to continue, since she was not a certified teacher. For anyone who knows Montez, though, they know she was a great teacher.

In 1972 God began putting in place the steps leading me

to bring my time as pastor at Turkey Creek to a close. In April we visited Dover Shores Baptist Church in Orlando, Florida, in view of a call, and I was led to accept the pastorate there. The first Friday night in June we attended the high school graduation ceremony for Jim and moved to Orlando the next morning.

Countless challenges confronted me during the time that I was pastor at Turkey Creek, but over the ten years that we were there we developed close friendships with many of the members that have stood the test of time. During my ministry there, I performed many weddings and watched as those couples had children and raised their families. I have gone back and preached three revivals. I have been asked to come back and conduct funerals for many of the church members from that time. From 2014 to 2020, I went back for six funerals, even though we had been gone for fifty years. While it was a challenging time, it was a very rewarding time as well. Many people came to salvation and were baptized. Many men grew up and were ordained to serve as deacons, then another half dozen were called to preach and ordained to the ministry. The church developed a strong Sunday School, had good choirs, had a bus ministry, offered Vacation Bible Schools, organized youth trips, hosted revivals, and sponsored the Pleasant Grove mission. It was a special time for me and my family. It was also a special time for many of the people in the community, and that bond has remained between them and us even all these years later.

5

DOVER SHORES YEARS

DOVER SHORES BAPTIST CHURCH WITH MY FAMILY.

ONE SUNDAY MORNING AT TURKEY CREEK, TWO LADIES visited the church. They were friendly and warmly welcomed. That night five men came and visited. We learned then that the two ladies and five men were a pulpit committee from Dover Shores Baptist Church in Orlando. They didn't say much other than that they enjoyed the service. I thought they had written us off. But I was curious, so I looked up information on the church. There was nothing very impressive about the church. I tried to forget about it.

The following Tuesday night I received a call from them. They were in a pulpit committee meeting. They had been impressed with the services and wanted to talk to me about possibly being their pastor. None of the members had experience on a committee like this. They didn't know how to proceed. I had to guide them along step by step. When I agreed to meet with them, I asked when I could expect them to come. They said they wanted Montez and me to come to Orlando.

We drove over to Orlando and met with them and had a good productive visit. One lady on the committee had made a delicious cola cake. I had never had any. It was so good I said in a kidding way, "Maybe we should come just to enjoy this kind of cake."

A few weeks later, we drove over again on a Sunday morning for me to preach and for us to meet with the people. That night I got an answer from God.

That was April 1972, and we requested a move date of June so our oldest could graduate at Turkey Creek High School. On the night of graduation, Jim gave a graduation speech, Dianne played in the high school band, and after it was over we went back to an empty parsonage. The movers had already come and gone, so we slept on the floor that night. Jim was going into the Air Force, so he would stay behind and live with one of the families in the church, the Pickerns. They had four boys, so one more would not be a problem. The next morning we packed up what was left into two cars and drove the seventy miles north to Orlando.

Just like when we went to Turkey Creek and learned how serious their problems were, so too we came to Dover Shores and then learned how serious *their* problems were.

1. The previous pastor had left very discouraged, saying, "I will never pastor another church."
2. The minister of youth, music, and education said the same. They resigned at the same time.
3. The interim music director said, "On the first day a new pastor comes will be my last Sunday." And it was.
4. The secretary left because they moved away.
5. In a few weeks, the pianist and organist both resigned.
6. I never saw or met the custodian, so after a few weeks I fired him.
7. I asked the Sunday School director what plans they had for reaching the community. He said, "My term is up in two months, and my plans are to resign then."

That was my welcome to Dover Shores. Despite all this, however, God began to move in the church. He gave us a minister of music and youth. He gave us outstanding musicians. He gave us an excellent custodian who always went above and beyond his agreed-upon responsibilities. We grew rapidly, and soon we were offering two morning worship services.

We soon saw the need for a new worship center. God led us all the way. We had a wonderful architect, Ed Thomas, who helped us tremendously. The same was true of the contractor, Gene Kelsey. In a later chapter, I will share some specific experiences of how God showed us just how closely he was leading us through this time of growth in the church.

Unfortunately, during the construction of the new sanctuary, we had a major tragedy. When the builders had dug the retention pond, they piled the dirt in a large mound. Three neighborhood boys were playing around the dirt pile on a late Wednesday afternoon. They decided to tunnel through from one side to the other. Two of the boys were near the midway point when the dirt pile caved in on them. Those two boys were trapped and died. Although the fire department, located at the end of the street, was there immediately, it was too late. Back then we had Wednesday-night supper before prayer meeting, and many of the members showed up for church that night having not even heard what had happened. The boys' families were not church people, so I did the funeral for them. It was a very difficult ordeal.

While we walked through that unimaginable tragedy and the challenges that come along with a building program, the church grew in many ways. The Wednesday-night suppers prior to prayer meeting proved to be a popular way to encourage fellowship, and prayer meeting attendance increased as well.

We also had outreach programs through sports. Just like Turkey Creek, we had incredible softball teams in both men's and women's leagues. This became an effective ministry to the men and women who were on the teams, and the games were a social outing for the church as well.

Some of the guys started getting together behind the church in the afternoon after Thanksgiving dinner to play football. Each year more and more would show up, and before we knew it we had the Turkey Bowl, an annual Dover Shores tradition. This grew to the point at which we had to have a men's game and a women's game, both being played at the same time, with the spectators sitting between the two games.

God continued to provide the right personnel at the right time. We were so blessed to have George and Teresa Atwell as our organist and pianist as well as choir leader. Their talent, along with Teresa's brother, Randy Nichols, on drums encouraged our youth to sing and play instruments when normally they would not have stepped out into that opportunity to grow.

Amazing individuals came forward to volunteer as chaperones willing to take our youth to Camp Joy, in Apopka. The youth group grew tremendously during this period.

Some families began to visit the church because they had heard about the top-notch nursery. They came for the nursery and stayed because of the spirit of the people in the church. We began a Mother's Day Out program, in which young moms could bring their children to the church one day a week so they could run errands, get to appointments, or just take a much-needed break.

As in any church, there were a lot of weddings and funerals, and Dover Shores was no exception. Besides the funeral for the boys who died at the construction site, one of the more significant funerals was for one of our neighbors, Mr. Harper. During the summer of 1973, Montez and I had driven out to Portland, Oregon, to the Southern Baptist Convention. We had dropped Dianne and Eric off in Memphis at Montez's parents' home. While we were at the convention, we received a call that Mr. Harper had been killed in an auto accident. We flew back to Orlando to conduct the funeral, then after the funeral, flew back to Portland. He was so special to us and our children that it was not a question of whether we would be there or not.

God was so good to us during those Dover Shores years. Dianne and Eric graduated from high school, and all three of my children served in the military. I was able to complete my doctorate from Luther Rice Seminary. The church grew tremendously in all the spiritual ways a pastor wants to see God bless his church—bless *his* church. In 1980 I felt God was calling me to move on. While there we made lifelong friends who continued to love and support us.

Next stop: director of missions (DOM) for the Greater Orlando Baptist Association.

6

DIRECTOR OF
MISSIONS TO PRESENT

CLEANING UP AROUND THE GREATER ORLANDO
BAPTIST ASSOCIATION (GOBA) OFFICE.

FROM THE EARLY TIMES OF MY MINISTRY, I BEGAN HAVING
a healthy respect for our Southern Baptist denomination. At

Leaf, my chairman of deacons was moderator of the Greene County Association. He helped me see the importance of this work. When we had been at Walnut Grove about two years, our missionary resigned. I was asked to take the position. I was honored but felt no leadership from God to accept.

When we were at Turkey Creek for about seven years, the missionary there resigned. The local association felt we did not need a missionary, but we would be led by a local moderator. Because of my involvement in the association, I was asked to become the moderator and acting association missionary. This was a great experience. I traveled to Ridgecrest, North Carolina, and Glorietta, New Mexico, our two national retreat centers. My family was exposed to these because they could travel with me.

When we had been at Dover Shores, our DOM, the new name for missionary, retired. I was called to be the new DOM of the GOBA. This calling process was not simple for several reasons: Our guidelines stated the candidate must have been an association leader. Leading pastors had recommended others for the position. They had been advised "don't call anyone locally." They had been advised "don't call a pastor."

Even though I felt it was God's will for me to accept, I was afraid that, for all the reasons listed above, I would not be called. When the vote was taken, it was unanimous to call me. That was God's intervention in a mighty way.

The GOBA had eighty-nine churches. This is the first level of our denominational organization. The next level is the Florida Baptist Convention (FBC), located in Jacksonville, Florida; then the Southern Baptist Convention, located in Nashville, Tennessee; and finally the Baptist World Alliance, located in Falls Church, Virginia. Many good things happened while we were there.

We had a contract with the Baptist Sunday School Board to sell bookstore products through our association office. This was okay for a while, but business grew rapidly, and we could not continue in our office. The Sunday School Board in Nashville, Tennessee, had put a moratorium on opening new bookstores. But because I was on the Sunday School Board, I had direct access to the director of the bookstore division. After many discussions, he agreed to make an exception, and they put in a full-fledged bookstore—the name was later changed to Lifeway Christian Bookstore. Ours became very profitable for them.

Another outstanding achievement was the founding of a center in Orlando for the New Orleans Baptist Seminary (NOBTS) Distance Learning Center. This center struggled but survived, and many people were able to do most of their seminary work here. This was a partnership between NOBTS, GOBA, the Baptist College of Florida and the FBC. Years later I had the opportunity to lead that center.

In 1983 Don Mott, a godly layman, and I worked together in inviting the Billy Graham Evangelistic Association to come to Orlando for a crusade. They accepted our invitation and came. The crusade was held in the Tangerine Bowl—a.k.a. the Citrus Bowl and now the Camping World Stadium. This was a tremendous challenge getting this event put together. It was a great blessing to work hand in hand with these godly men, and the crusade was quite a success.

In this job, I counseled pastors, did various types of training, started new churches, and preached two, three, or four times on Sunday. I mostly preached at churches throughout GOBA whose pastor was either sick or on vacation or was not available for whatever reason. One Sunday I was filling in for a pastor who was on vacation, and there was a couple there. I didn't know them, so I didn't know if they were visiting or already members of that church. Soon after I got up to preach, the man had a heart attack. The EMTs came and worked on him and took him to the hospital. His wife stayed at church and didn't go with him. Well, that seemed odd to me, but since it appeared she wasn't going to be going anywhere anytime soon, I resumed preaching. I finished and gave the invitation. The wife immediately came forward and said, "We come to move our letters from somebody else's church." And that explained that!

When I started this work with GOBA, Montez tried

going with me as I preached at a different church each week. Of course, I was loving it, but soon she said, "I don't like this. You are serving; I am doing nothing." She wanted to go back to Dover Shores and work in the nursery. This was her strongest point and her passion, so that is what she did.

One highlight was that one year I was invited to go to Australia on a preaching crusade. Charles Gentry, formerly from Dover Shores, organized the details of the trip. Jim Wilson, a full-time evangelist, led crusades in many countries.

When we landed in Brisbane, Australia, a large crowd had gathered to be there when our plane landed. We wondered why we had such a large crowd to welcome us. We were excited for great things to happen with this kind of welcome. It turned out that Boy George, a rock star, was on our plane, and they were there to welcome him!

I preached in four different churches during those two weeks. Some extracurricular highlights were going to a local sheepshearing barn. It was fun watching these men shear the sheep. We also went to the outback to visit a large tomato farm. There were hundreds of acres of tomatoes in one field. I had remembered only those grown in a garden.

∞

In 1985 I received a call from Dr. Jim Goodson, at the FBC. He asked if I would consider coming to the convention in Jacksonville, Florida, as director of the New Work Assistance department. Dr. Dan Stringer was the executive director of the state convention. After meeting with them, I felt God leading me to accept the offer. I had been very happy as the DOM in Orlando and did not want to leave, but I felt God calling. The vote by the State Board of Missions was unanimous, so we moved to Jacksonville.

This job required that I travel a lot. My area of work was the entire state of Florida, from Pensacola to Key West—the distance between these two cities is *further* than the distance between Pensacola and Chicago, Illinois. I had the responsibility of providing grants to churches buying property or a building for a new church. I had to obtain a real estate license for this job, which was a challenge as well. We also made low-interest loans for older churches needing money. I was the loan officer for the convention. I would prepare all the paperwork for the proper committees to approve the loan or grant. I continually traveled throughout the state with not only my regular duties but also the opportunity to preach all over the state as well. During the ten years I was at the convention, I served as interim pastor at five different churches. This was a real joy because I was still a pastor at heart, even though I was in denominational work.

ONE OF OUR CHURCHES IN BIG SKY COUNTRY (MONTANA).

I also traveled to North Dakota, South Dakota, and Montana. These trips were because Florida was partnered with the Baptists in these states, where the work was not as robust as in the southern and western states. Later we established a partnership with Pennsylvania, so I went there to work with them a few times.

Eventually, we were partnered with Tanzania, in East Africa. My trip there was unusual. The FBC had brought a little boy to Jacksonville to get a prosthesis because a crocodile had bitten his arm off at the elbow. When it was time for him to return home, I was asked to take him. On the day we were to leave, we were at the airport an hour and a half ahead of our departure. Their computer system was shut down, and they were doing everything by hand. By the time they had us processed, our plane had left. This was a major concern because all our flight connections had been set. Finally, we got another flight to LaGuardia, in New York City. In the middle of the night, I had to find transportation to John F. Kennedy International. God provided a Christian chauffer to take us.

We arrived in Amsterdam around ten the next morning and met the rest of our team. They had been afraid we were lost somewhere—this was before cell phones, so it was pretty much a guessing game as to what was going on. We all arrived safely in Dar es Salaam and were greeted by our missionaries there. After eating a delicious supper of wildebeest and resting that night, we were taken across country to Mbeya, a large city in western Tanzania. There we met missionaries and local church leaders. This trek took all day. I had sent money from the FBC for the people to purchase tin for church roofs. The local churches there had to make their own building blocks and build the walls of the new churches. They had to have the tin for the roofs on hand. They also had to have poles we could use for making rafters. The next day we drove over the worst mountain roads I had ever traveled on. We arrived at our first church. Our team of five, consisting of three missionaries and two locals, began to build rafters, put them on the buildings, and nail tin on the roofs.

We finished the first church in one day. Old men in their culture did not work; they sat and watched. The large crowd who gathered were very surprised that I, a sixty-two-year-old gray-haired man, was working alongside the others. I was very, very tired at the end of the day—those old men were smart to just sit and watch. The next day was Sunday. I preached at the main church at eight o'clock in the morning. This was an English service, so I needed no translator. Next I preached to a new congregation at ten at a schoolhouse; then I preached at the main church at eleven. This service was unusual. The building held around one hundred people here in the United States. They packed about five hundred into that building. Then we walked two miles to a deacon's house for lunch. After the long day of travel over rough roads, working another long day building the church, preaching three services, and then walking two miles to lunch, I was very, very, very tired.

We built four more churches while we were there. I stayed and preached and led conferences after the other team members left to come home. On my trip home, we stopped briefly in Nairobi, Kenya, then on to Amsterdam, where I had a half-day layover. Among other things, I took the boat ride on the canals. I was surprised to see that many of the streets were canals.

Later the FBC partnered with the Caribbean Baptist Fellowship. This was a convention made up of churches scattered throughout the Caribbean. I went to several islands and visited their churches. While I was there, I was invited to come back and preach a revival in Dominica. That was a delightful experience.

A major challenge for all of us at the convention was in 1992, when Hurricane Andrew came through South Florida. While all convention workers were involved in some way, my job was to help churches restore their buildings, or in some cases completely rebuild. I was down there—back and forth—for two years. One of our biggest challenges in rebuilding was the incredible amount of fraud and price gouging that was rampant during that time. It did not seem to matter that this was for houses of worship.

I was interim pastor at Fellowship Baptist Church

in Madison, Florida, for ten months. I had helped this church get a loan and grant when they had started. Part of my schedule was that I would work in my office on Monday. I would leave early Tuesday morning to drive to South Florida, an approximately five-hour drive. I usually worked fourteen hours a day through Thursday. On Friday I would work there until five in the evening, then drive back to Jacksonville. On Saturday I would do what was necessary around the house—think "honey-do" list. On Sunday morning I would drive the 120 miles to Madison, preach the morning and evening services then drive back to Jacksonville that night. It was a long ten months, but God was good. I was grateful to Hal Mayer and his family for letting me live with them in South Florida during much of my time during the hurricane relief.

In 1992 Montez and I moved back to Orlando in anticipation of our retirement years. I worked at the convention another two and a half years before retiring in 1995. I am grateful for the people I worked with at the convention during the ten years I was there, and it was a joy and privilege to work for Dr. John Sullivan, who served as executive director after Dr. Stringer retired.

Before I had finished at the convention, the NOBTS Extension Center in Orlando needed a new director. I was called to serve there. We had no office and no secretary. We had to set up an office in our home. Montez was my secretary. It was a delight to work with the seminary leadership: Dr. Jimmy Dukes and Dr. Landrum Leavell. It was also a joy to work with these young—and not so young—men preparing for their God-called ministries. I started there in June 1995. In January 1996, I was called as interim pastor of Eastside Baptist Church, now Oasis at Conway Gardens.

EASTSIDE BAPTIST CHURCH.

Now in my "retirement," I was working harder than I had before, directing the center and pastoring the church. I also did contract work for two departments at the convention. One was conflict management for churches, and one was fundraising for churches.

One of these was different than the others. I was asked to go to a church in West Central Florida to help them to "rewrite their bylaws." I went to meet with them and saw right away they didn't need to rewrite their bylaws; they needed a full-fledged conflict-management engagement. They were in conflict and in trouble. I spent a few weeks helping them through that. A few years later, I was leading a statewide conference on fundraising for buildings. In one of the sessions, I saw three men from the church I had helped. They were there because they needed a new building. After a discussion with them, I learned that after the conflict management a few years before they began to grow and now needed another building. I explained that I did fundraising as well. They asked me to come for that project too.

We had a very good experience with the seminary but could not continue, because the church was growing as well as the seminary. The workload was too much, so we resigned from the work at the seminary after fourteen months. Even though I was interim at Eastside while they searched for a pastor, I was working pretty much full time at the church, so the church just dropped the interim title.

INTERIM TITLE REMOVED FROM THE MARQUEE.

After more than three very good years at Eastside, our DOM at GOBA resigned. This was in 1999. The Southern Baptist Convention was coming to Orlando in 2000 for their annual meeting. Preparations for their arrival required much leadership and a lot of hard work. Because I had experience as DOM here before, I was asked to come lead the association, at least through the convention meeting. We left Eastside and came back to GOBA and hit the ground running.

We had a lot of help from the North American Mission Board. Among many highlights of the convention coming to Orlando was a Unified Language Churches Evangelism event. We brought together all our foreign language church pastors to plan strategies for evangelism. I soon became amazed at the high energy level of these men. We had Hispanic, Haitian, Filipino, Korean, Chinese, and Vietnamese pastors. A very big evangelistic crusade for all languages was held at the Central Florida Fairgrounds. It was a full carnival atmosphere with a spiritual emphasis. Hundreds of people came to the rally. Music, testimonies, and preaching were well done. During the invitation, one lady—among many—came and accepted Christ. We also had a drawing to give away a car. We had raised money to buy a good Toyota. After the service was over, we brought in the car. When the drawing was held, and the winning number was drawn, it was the lady who was just saved earlier in the evening. She left that rally blessed beyond all measure.

While I was at GOBA the second time, the state convention had partnered with the Baptist Convention of Belgium. I wanted us, as an association, to join in this partnership as well. That partnership—and the trip to Belgium—was another highlight of my time during this second go-round.

While we were at GOBA, Montez became very ill. Soon it was apparent my primary responsibility needed to be at home. During this time my own health began to decline. In 2002 I "retired" the second time. Montez's illness went into remission, and her health began to improve.

After leaving GOBA my health improved a little. I preached regularly. One time was special. I got a call from a church in Key West. They wanted me to come train their pastor search committee. Montez and I drove down on Saturday. I preached on Sunday; we had a relaxing time for the next week. I worked with the church some during the week and preached the next Sunday. We came home on Monday. I went back about a month later. It was a great experience.

In January 2003, I went as part-time pastor of First Baptist Church of Winter Springs.

WINTER SPRINGS.

The church had a building debt that was impossible to pay. They had just gone through a church split. About one-third of the people—and finances—left. I saw no way sixty people could pay $8,000 per month with just those few individuals. I told the congregation that survival could not happen with the best human efforts—only a miracle from God could save the church. Amazingly, God worked several miracles, the church survived, and God blessed them greatly. We had many conversions. It was interesting when I told people that I baptized in the kitchen table. We had no baptistry. The kitchen table consisted of a large vat on rollers. It had a granite covering, making it a functional table. When we baptized, we rolled it into the sanctuary. The covering was removed, and it was filled with water. One of the people I baptized was in his seventies. I led him to the Lord in his home. He later became the head usher. Another man I led to the Lord while visiting his home became the chairman of deacons. God was working miracles in his house.

KITCHEN-TABLE BAPTISM.

I retired from Winter Springs in September 2004, technically retirement number three. In the late fall of 2004, the doctors finally diagnosed my health problems. I had atrial fibrillation; cardiomyopathy; and valve regurgitation, which consists of bleeding around the valve inside the heart. We tried medication to cure it, but it did not work. On April 26, 2005, they did the heart valve repair surgery. They had to take the heart out of my body, repair the valves, and put it back in. I had a whole new appreciation for my granddaughter Amy, who had had three open heart surgeries by the age of ten. I was in the hospital longer than expected. I eventually made a full recovery—so I could have a full knee replacement the following year.

In September 2006, Dover Shores Baptist Church was without a pastor. We were asked to come help them until they could find an interim pastor. We went. God blessed us, and in November *they called me* as interim. In January I decided the church needed someone full time, so I began to work full time. Once again God worked miracles, and we grew. In May 2007, I was called as full-time senior pastor. We served until August 21, 2011. My retirement date was on my eightieth birthday. This was my fourth retirement. By then my children had stopped giving me retirement gifts!

FOURTH RETIREMENT, BUT NOT TO BE MY LAST!

JAMES AND MONTEZ.

When we left Dover Shores, we began attending First Baptist Church of Orlando. We thoroughly enjoyed our small group fellowship. Our leaders were Paul and Jean Waters, who had served with us the first time we were at Dover Shores in the seventies. After two years there, I was asked to join the staff as minister on call. That ministry consisted mostly of comforting the sick, visiting nursing homes, conducting funerals, and other needs. A dedicated staff was needed to fulfill the needs of a church the size of FBC. One day while I was on call, a man called into the church. He wanted me to warn David Uth, our senior pastor, that Jesus was coming back. I said, "Okay, I agree with you. When is he coming?"

The man said, "This Sunday morning at about eight thirty."

I asked, "Where will he come?"

He said, "My driveway."

I assured the man that I would pass that on to the pastor.

Another interesting incident happened when I was asked to go to Davenport to perform a funeral. Something did not seem right. After the service, as people were leaving, I heard shouting. It seems there was a major conflict between the deceased man's wife and his girlfriend. That was the most difficult funeral service I ever experienced.

In 2014 I was called to South Conway Road Baptist Church as pastor. This was our first church ever that did not have Sunday-evening services. That was okay because

I was getting older—now eighty-three years old. We had four adults saved, and I baptized six altogether. One was a six-eight man who weighed about 280 pounds. He was very heavy for me to baptize, but we made it. We stayed eighteen months, then the church united with another congregation and called their pastor to lead the new united church. Retirement number five—I'm wearing them like Tom Brady Super Bowl rings now.

After a year I was asked to come to Shenandoah Baptist Church to serve as interim pastor. Dover Shores had begun sponsoring Shenandoah back in the 1970s, and one of the leading laymen, Ed Carpenter, had served faithfully with his family all those years. It was a real blessing to reunite with Ed and his family. Another reunion was with the worship leader, Rex Terrell, with whom I had served at a church a few years prior to this. Along with these men, there were a number of other excellent Bible teachers and church workers at Shenandoah. One lady, who was eighty-three years old, accepted Christ, and our youth minister baptized her. We were there fifteen months before they called their next pastor. Retirement number six.

In my postretirement years, I still take every opportunity to preach. I thank God that he has given me the strength to continue to preach his word. I still conduct funerals when asked. It has also been a blessing to be able to host a men's Bible study in my community, Ventura, mostly with men whom I see on the golf course. I never wanted to retire to take up the rocking chair to just sit around. I am so grateful that as my years as a pastor and association and convention staff member have concluded God has still provided me with opportunities to preach, teach, and minister to his people.

7

SPIRITUAL PILGRIMAGE

IN THIS SECTION, I WOULD LIKE TO REVISIT SOME EXPERIENCES noted above from the perspective of my spiritual progression.

I was always interested in going to church when I had a chance. When I was twelve, I went to a Pentecostal church near where we lived. I joined the church and was baptized in a lake. Everything they told me to do, I did, so I thought I was saved. They also taught that if I sinned I would be lost again. Of course, I sinned—as everyone does, according to the Bible—so I was "lost" again.

When we moved to Mississippi, I started going to a small church, where the congregation was both Baptist and Methodist and would gather in the same service. One week a Baptist preacher would preach, and the next week a Methodist preacher would preach. Baptists taught "once saved, always saved," but I knew better because of what happened to me at the Pentecostal church. I would have to walk about two and a half miles to get to church. Sometimes one of my siblings would go with me, or sometimes a neighbor. The church building had one room. The heat was a big potbellied stove, and the toilets were outside.

The church had four Sunday School classes. We met in each corner of the church. The youth department was usually two people: me and one other. The one other was usually someone different every week.

We had a revival each August. The first Sunday of the revival we would have dinner on the grounds—a really big event. In 1948, during the revival, I was under heavy conviction to accept Christ. I resisted, though I'm not sure why. On Wednesday or Thursday night, Leonard went forward to make a decision, but I still resisted. That night the evangelist preached on the Second Coming of Christ. He used the passage "two will be in the field, one will be taken and the other left" (Matthew 24:40). The next day Leonard and I were plowing cotton in the same field. The presence of the Holy Spirit was very strong on me. Each time I plowed a row, I would see Leonard, and the verse "one will be taken and the other left" would press down on me. I could just see he would be taken, and I would be left. About two o'clock in the afternoon, I could stand it no longer. I stopped my mule and prayed, asking God to forgive me and save me. Immediately the burden was lifted. I was free! I had real joy in my heart—peace I had not known.

I could hardly wait to get to church that night. During the service, I could hardly wait for the invitation. Previously I had dreaded the invitation because of my burden of sin. I stepped out on the very first word and went forward. I told the preacher what had happened. Then I said I didn't want to be baptized, because I had been already. Once I had heard a Pentecostal preacher brag that he had been baptized seven times, and that really turned me off. The pastor listened to me and then counseled me. His total counsel was, "We don't take them like that. You need to be baptized."

I said okay, and then he asked if I wanted to join the Baptist or Methodist church—a common question for that situation. I said Baptist. Leonard, Luther, and I were all baptized in the Sunflower River soon thereafter.

By the time I was in the twelfth grade, when questions were asked about the Bible or when an occasion came for prayer, I was the one they called on. I'm not sure if any of my classmates were born-again Christians, although some were church members. Ours was a good moral group. There weren't any "bad apples" among us.

One summer I went to school at Mississippi College, a Baptist college near Jackson. One day, while I was sitting in class, I had a sudden frightening feeling all over. A presence said, "You're going to be a preacher." Of course, that had to be wrong. I could never be a preacher; I was going to be a football coach. I gave God all the reasons why this could never happen. A few days went by, and I got over it. When the semester was over, I went back to Hattiesburg. Soon the same feeling came again. I used the same argument. About three weeks later, the same feeling again. This time it didn't go away. I was losing my mind! About three o'clock in the morning, when I could not sleep, I prayed and told God that if he would always go with me, then I would be a preacher. Peace came then.

When I went to Southern Miss, I became active in the First Baptist Church in Hattiesburg. This was my cousin Letha's church. I also became active in the BSU, of which I was elected president.

There was a meeting coming up in Starkville, about one hundred miles away, and the state BSU president and I decided we would leave early and hitchhike up there. Our plan didn't work out so well. We had great difficulty catching a ride and ended up being very late instead of very early.

Our church had a policy that if one of their members was elected president of the BSU the church would pay fifty dollars to send them to Ridgecrest, a Baptist retreat in

North Carolina. My BSU director was taking me there for Student Week. At that time I had been invited to preach at a church nearby. They paid me twenty-five dollars each week. On Saturday night, before leaving for Ridgecrest on Monday, I spent the night with Letha and her family. I was very excited about this tremendous trip.

On Saturday night I got sick. By Sunday morning, before church, I was very sick. Letha knew a doctor in the church. She called him and explained the situation. He told her to bring me to the hospital immediately. We met him at eight. He examined me and said I had an appendicitis and had to have surgery. Now I was torn; I was going to Ridgecrest the next day. He said, "No, you're not. You must have it removed now." I had the surgery and missed the trip. He told me later that my appendix would have burst within the next hour if it had not been removed. Back then that was almost a death sentence.

The doctor didn't charge me anything. I offered to give back the money to the church, but they said keep it. With that fifty dollars and the fifty dollars from preaching, I paid the full hospital bill. A few years later, this same doctor delivered my son Jim.

Those years in Hattiesburg presented a lot of challenges, but I can never say enough about how much Letha and her family meant to me. They made my life much better during my time at Southern.

Does God still speak to us today?

This is a frequently discussed question. Many mature Christians still say no. Part of this issue is semantics. Different people interpret the question in different ways. I say the answer is yes and will share several instances in which God clearly spoke to me.

1. My call to preach, which was described above, was the main one.

2. In another instance, I was having car trouble and took the car to a dealer for repair. While I was there, a salesman showed me a car he wanted to sell me. He was persuasive. God said, "Don't buy it." The salesman won out, though, and I bought the car. On my way home, the car stopped! The radiator had run dry, so the car had overheated and badly damaged the engine. The dealer who sold it would not take the care of it. I wound up paying $142 to repair it, which was a fortune at that time.

3. God spoke to me again after I left the first church I pastored and went back to school. I left on good terms, not because of anything negative or derogatory, but I was exhausted from driving over 240 miles every other weekend, so I needed to give up preaching at this church. After about six weeks, God spoke to me and said, "Go back to Cagle's Crossing." I explained to the Lord that:

- That was impossible.
- I just couldn't do that.
- It won't work out.
- They probably didn't want me.

He said, "You write them and say you are willing to come back." I was out on the street praying.

Around two in the morning, I said, "I will write them." I thought they would laugh at me and say no thanks. When they received the letter, and it was read on Sunday morning, there were lots of amens, and that morning they voted unanimously to call me back.

4. The pulpit committee from Turkey Creek had come to Walnut Grove, and we had agreed I would come down for the trial sermon. Before I had been down and didn't know much about the church, I prayed for God's will to be revealed. While I was praying one day, God said, "You're going to Florida." When they voted for us, the call was one hundred percent.

5. At Turkey Creek, one Saturday night I was in my study, praying for the service the next day. God spoke to me and said, "Go and see Mr. Golden."

I said, "All right, Lord, I will go first thing next week."

God said, "No, you go now and see him." Mr. Golden had a little country store. I told God I didn't know where he lived and that the store was probably closed. God said, "Go now!" and I went. When I got to the store, it was still open. Customers kept coming in, which prevented me from speaking to Mr. Golden, and after about a thirty-minute wait I was getting frustrated. A man came in the store, and Mr. Golden introduced us. I began talking to him, and soon I could see the Holy Spirit was working on him. We went out to the car, and he prayed to receive Christ. Only God knew he would be there and sent me there at the right time.

6. Paul Broadway had grown up in the same community with Floyd Higginbotham and me. He was saved in the same church, had been called to preach, and was a pastor in Mississippi. I had the privilege of preaching four revivals at his churches. One day Floyd called me and said Paul was in a car accident and was not expected to live. He went on to tell me that I needed to pray for his wife and children. I immediately began to pray. God spoke and said, "This kind goes out by nothing but by prayer and fasting." God was saying, "Pray and fast."

I told God "I can't fast. I have tried lots of times." But God's word was there to stay. This was about two o'clock in the afternoon. I prayed but didn't eat anything. About two o'clock the next afternoon,

God spoke again, "Paul will be well soon. You can go eat now." Paul recovered, and I preached two more revivals for him.

7. We were contacted by First Baptist Church of Saint Cloud, Florida, about coming on as pastor. We went and preached the trial sermon. The building was beautiful. The congregation was larger than what we had at Turkey Creek. The prospects for a fruitful ministry appeared promising. As the service proceeded, before I got up to preach, God said, "These are fine people, but they are not yours. You don't come here." I had to decline the call to that church.

8. When we were contacted about going to Dover Shores Baptist Church in Orlando, we came for the trial sermon. The situation was not ideal; the church had many problems. That night, back at Turkey Creek, I had a prayer meeting with a small group, as we did regularly. During that prayer meeting, God said, "You are going to Orlando."

9. At Dover Shores we had a lady who joined the church. Everyone loved her. When she was diagnosed with cancer, we prayed for her. The cancer went into remission. One day I was in my office praying for her, and God spoke. "Tell her to put her house in order because she will die and not live long."

I was crushed. I prayed, "God, please give the right words and the right time to talk to her."

He said, "Go now."

I reluctantly went to her apartment. Two of her close friends were there. They were in the Charismatic movement and believed in faith healing. I groaned inside and said to myself, "Oh no." I immediately told her what God said, then left.

About a month later, after church one night, I got a call from the lady. She was in the hospital and needed to see me. I went there, and she said, "I won't make it. I need to do what you said and get my house in order." She shared with me some things that needed to be settled. We prayed, and she was at peace about going to heaven. She died a few weeks later.

10. God blessed our work at Dover Shores, and soon we needed to build a new building. We made all the plans and began saving money. When we had the plans ready to present to the church, we were apprehensive about how we would pay for it. As I was preparing the sermon for the Sunday we were to vote, I came to Isaiah 54:2–3: "Enlarge the place of your tent; stretch out the curtains of your dwellings, spare not; lengthen your cords and strengthen your stakes."

God spoke and said, "There is your answer."

I said, "Lord, I understand, but what will happen if we can't make the payments?"

Then I read verse 4: "Fear not for you will not be put to shame." When the building was almost finished, and a date for opening was set, we faced a dilemma. We had borrowed money to build the building but had decided to do everything else as money was given. The music committee found the piano and organ we needed. They couldn't order them, because we had to have the money first. The organ had to be custom built to our building and would take three months to build. We decided to continue to use the old piano and wait for the money to get the new piano and organ. Six weeks went by. One Sunday morning I woke up early, and God spoke to me and said, "If you will ask me, I will give you the piano and organ for opening day."

I explained that could not happen, because it would take three months to build it, and we only had seven weeks left before we were ready to move into the new building.

He repeated, "You ask me, and I will do it."

I said, "All right, Lord, I am asking you to do it."

God said, "No, you tell the congregation what I will do."

I felt good about asking God about it. But if I told the church, and it didn't happen, that would be embarrassing. God said, "You must tell them." At the early service—we held two morning services in the current sanctuary—I shared what had happened. At the invitation I asked all those who would pray and ask for the piano and organ to come and kneel to pray. Most of the people came.

After the prayer, people came to me and said, "God just told me to give a certain amount of money." The same thing happened during the second service. We wound up with enough money and pledges to pay for them. We still had the problem of three months to build the organ and seven weeks to do it. The committee went back to the store to place the order. They were told it would be ready on time. What had happened was when the committee had gone early on in the process the people started building it, but we didn't know that. We started in the new building with the new piano and the new organ.

11. While at Dover Shores, I was going to the pastors' fellowship meeting one morning. Near the church where we were meeting, I stopped for a red light. While waiting for the light to change, I saw a hippie standing there, hitchhiking. God said, "Pick him up."

I said, "I can't. I'm only going a little ways."

"Pick him up!" the Lord repeated.

After several seconds of arguing with God, I picked him up. There was no time for lifestyle evangelism. I asked him about his relationship with

God. He said, "I believe in God, and I believe in Jesus, but I don't believe in churches, and I don't believe in preachers."

I talked with him about Jesus, and after about forty minutes he prayed and accepted Christ. I missed the pastor's meeting that day. I dropped him off where he worked. He agreed to come to church on Sunday, if he had a way to get there. My chairman of deacons went to get him, took him to breakfast, and brought him to church. At church he still looked like a hippie—and smelled like one too. When I gave the invitation, he came forward. He wanted the people to know he was saved but didn't want to join the church. He continued to attend and rode his ten-speed bike. About three months later, he came forward during the invitation again. He said, "I did not know people could love me. I want to be baptized and join the church." Several years later a businessman in a three-piece suit, with his lovely wife, visited the church. I introduced myself. He said, "I'm Jim Lawrence." The former hippie had become a real estate broker and had moved to Massachusetts.

I would like to share some other memories outside the times in which God has spoken to me. There were plenty of highlights while we were at Walnut Grove, and I would like to share one that is related to a family.

A little boy, Wayne, was invited by his friend to come to RAs. He kept coming, and I would take him home afterward. He lived a few miles out of town.

One day I was ready to tell him I could not continue to take him home, as it was costly for me. On the day I was going to talk to him, it was raining, and we had to wait at the church for a while. During the wait he accepted Christ. I felt bad that I had considered telling him I could not continue to drive him home. That day I met his mother and grandparents to tell them about Wayne. The grandfather was in the latter stages of Alzheimer's disease.

A few weeks later, the grandmother called me one Saturday morning. She asked if I could come to see her husband. He was lucid and alert. I took the Methodist pastor with me, which was what we did in those days, and we went to see him. He was alert, and we talked freely. That morning he accepted Christ. By noon his mind was gone again.

After that he couldn't recognize me. But when I visited him, he always had a story to tell. Once he said, "Mister, let me tell you something. I was in my barn, and it was falling down on me. These two fellas came and talked to me. After that I was fine."

Another story he told: "Mister, I was down at my pond, and I was falling in and drowning. These two fellas came and talked to me, and now I am fine."

Several months later I received a phone call that he had

died. He was eighty-nine years old. His daughter told me, "Last night, about midnight, he woke up, and his mind was perfectly clear. He pointed up to the ceiling and said, 'Heaven is up there, and I'm going there.' He died within two hours."

Another event is related to the greatest revival service I was ever in. We had scheduled a revival that most of the people didn't want. The next week progressed, and very little was happening. Someone from another church said, "I heard nobody is paying attention to it." That broke my heart, partly because I was doing the preaching! I was also leading the music.

On Thursday night I shared my burden. I asked the people to promise to pray at least thirty minutes before the next night. More than half of the people committed themselves to pray. The next day, Friday, it was raining. I needed to make several visits but could not. I needed to prepare a sermon but could not. No verse of scripture would come. I sat in my office and prayed and cried.

Church time came, and I still had no sermon. I told myself it was okay—it was raining, and no one would come. It was time for the service to start, and people began arriving. Despite the rain, they kept coming. We usually had around 100 people on Sunday morning. There, on a rainy Friday night, about 150 people came.

I was confused. I had no sermon. The music was being led by me. We had a great crowd—and in the rain, no less.

Still no sermon came. Finally, I said to the congregation, "I'm so sorry. I have no sermon." I spoke for about five minutes and gave the invitation. People started coming forward. They gathered around the front and knelt to pray. Soon they started to fill the nearby Sunday School rooms. Different people came to me to be saved or to make other decisions. The invitation lasted an hour and a half.

After about forty-five minutes, the man known as the town drunk got up, came to the front, and accepted Christ. He had not been in a church for thirty years.

There was a special, awesome atmosphere. God was so real and so present. Never before or since have I felt that Spirit. God can take a lot of worthless nothing and make a wonderful something out of it.

Another time I was in Mississippi at the Pleasant Hill Baptist Church, where my lifelong friend, Floyd Higginbotham, was pastor. The revival was to start on Sunday morning. On the Friday before, a man in the community was terminated from his job. He was hurt, angry, and distraught. That night he decided that on Monday morning he was going back to the place where he had worked to kill those involved, and then he would kill himself.

On Saturday morning men from the church were out visiting in the community, inviting people to church. They came to the house of this man and invited him to church the next day—opening day of the revival. The man said to himself, "This is my last Sunday on earth, so I might as well go to church." He was not a churchgoer.

On Sunday morning he came. The people had no idea what had happened to him on Friday or what he had planned for the next day. During the service God did a wonderful thing in his heart. When I gave the invitation, he came forward and gave his life to Christ. Of course, his plans for Monday never came to fruition.

Soul Winning

There have been many debates about the term *soul winning*. I will use it in the context that one person shares Christ with another. The person who hears it then accepts Christ.

When I had been saved, we had another revival. The evangelist asked, "How long has it been since you led someone to Christ? A week? A month? A year?"

I got convicted. I had been a Christian for an entire year and had not led anyone to Christ. Years went by, and I had not led anyone to Christ personally. I would preach, and people would get saved, but one-on-one witnessing was not occurring. I was burdened about this. One day I shared this burden with a friend. He gave me a book, *Soul*

Winning Made Easy by C. S. Lovett. I studied it carefully, and through the instructions provided I began leading people to Christ.

I kept a fairly good record of the people who accepted Christ. By the time I finished my full-time ministry at age eighty, I had led more than twelve hundred to Christ. Since then, there were four at South Conway Baptist Church, one at Shenandoah Baptist Church, and one at Dover Shores Baptist Church. I can't share all those experiences, but I will relate a few here.

1. The first night I went out visiting I used that plan of salvation as taught in the Lovett book. The man I shared with prayed to receive Christ right there. When he finished praying, his wife had been listening and began to cry. I asked what was wrong, and she said, "Brother Fortinberry, I am not satisfied." She explained she had joined the church as a girl but didn't understand then what she was doing. She prayed to receive Christ. The next week I went back to the house to discuss their baptism. His twin brother and his wife were there. I shared the Gospel with them. They both accepted Christ, and I got to baptize all four of them.

2. I was preaching a revival for Paul Broadway, whom I had witnessed to and led to Christ. During the

revival his wife, a lifelong church member, realized she was not saved. She accepted Christ. In my ministry, I led three pastors' wives and one pastor to Christ. That week Paul and I visited a man. We witnessed to him for two hours. He resisted the Holy Spirit. When he had said his final no, his wife, who had been listening, began to cry. She accepted Christ—he would not.

3. My son Eric injured his arm while at school. His coach thought he should go to the emergency room. He called and asked my permission. I said yes and said I would meet him there. On the way I prayed and gave thanks for everything. I didn't know why I should give thanks. Eric's arm might've been broken. When I got there and sat in the waiting room while he was examined, I met a lady. I shared Christ with her, and she accepted Christ. Then I knew why I should give thanks. Eric's arm was bruised but not broken. The next week I went to the home of the lady and met her husband. He accepted Christ that night. I baptized them both.

4. We had Vacation Bible School, and one of those who accepted Christ was a twelve-year-old boy. I went to his home to talk to him about his decision and baptism. When I explained the plan of salvation, it

was obvious he fully understood. The next afternoon I was leaving a hospital after visiting someone there. As I was leaving, I met the mother of the boy from the previous night. I asked her about why she was there. Her husband, the boy's father, had had a heart attack. There, in front of the hospital, with people coming and going, I asked her if she had thought any more about what we had discussed the night before. She said, "I have not thought about anything else." I asked if she was ready to receive Christ. She said yes. Right then, right there, she prayed and received Christ. She went up to see her husband and told him what she had done. She told him, "I'm going to church Sunday to make this public."

He said, "If you will wait one more week, I'll go with you." They came together. Later they told me that before I came to their home they had planned to get a divorce. Needless to say, the divorce did not happen.

5. One afternoon, before a previously scheduled meeting that night, I needed to see two people in two different hospitals. I didn't have time to go see both men before my meeting, so I thought I would go see the young man facing surgery the next day. I went to the hospital, but we could not find him, even with the nurses' help. He wasn't in his room.

Later I found out he had gone for more tests before his surgery. I looked at my watch and decided I had time to go see the other man at the other hospital across town. I went to his room and was able to share Christ with him, and he received Christ right then. Before midnight that night, the man who received Christ died. God knew what I didn't, so he made it possible for me to see him. The next morning the young man had his surgery. He, too, accepted Christ.

6. I went to see a man at his home. His wife was a Christian and member of our church. When I got there, I tried to witness to him. He was not interested at all. His niece was there visiting from Miami. The man got up and went to bed. I shared Christ with the niece. She said she wanted to be saved when I asked her to pray with me. We started with "Lord Jesus ..."

She could not say "Lord Jesus ..." We tried two or three times. She could not say it. I realized there was a satanic presence there. I prayed and asked God to remove this evil presence. Then we prayed again, and she prayed sincerely for God to save her. He did. I discussed baptism. She said she could not be baptized. In discussing this, I learned she had been a member of the Hell's Angels motorcycle gang. She had witnessed the crucifixion of a girl. She had been on drugs and caught up in all the things in that lifestyle. She continued to have problems. She would have terrible nightmares. She felt she was almost physically attacked by evil spirits. One day I was talking to her and noticed she had on rings that didn't seem right. One had a satanic emblem on it, and she said she had stolen the other at a store at Disney World. I told her she must destroy the satanic ring and take the other one back to the store. She did what I asked. After that she was free. She then wanted to be baptized. She went back to Miami and reconciled with her mother. Many years later I was on staff at First Baptist Church in Orlando. I did hospital visits. One day I was given the name of a patient in the hospital. I went and introduced myself. She said, "I know you." She was the one I had led to Christ in her uncle's home years before. I learned she had begun to serve the Lord. She had married a Christian man, and they were active at FBC Orlando.

7. While I worked for the FBC, we lived in Jacksonville. We had a problem with a church in Fort Myers. I had to go deal with it. I decided I could drive down in five hours, allow two hours for work, and drive home in another five hours. Not bad for us who worked there; we were used to long hours. I drove

down and arrived at noon. Instead of two hours, the problem took eight hours! By eight o'clock that night, I started home, tired, exhausted, and drained. An hour or so later, I had to stop for gas. I filled the tank and went in the store to pay for it. Two young women were there. One worked there, and the other was a friend of hers. I started witnessing to them. One was not interested; the other was interested. She prayed to receive Christ. She said she would tell her mother first. The mother and her Sunday school class had been praying for her for years. I drove the next four hours without getting tired or sleepy. I thought of John chapter 4, when Jesus wouldn't eat. He said he had food we don't know about.

Obviously, there were many more—to God be the glory! The ones I have shared are meant to show what he can do. We can only introduce people to Christ and tell them how to accept him. The entire salvation experience is a transaction between the person and Christ.

Plan of Salvation

For anyone who has a desire to accept Christ but is unsure how to proceed, the following steps will be most helpful. It is better to have a Bible in hand, but it is not necessary.

Step One

Read Romans 3:23: "For all have sinned and fall short of the glory of God." Notice *all*—that includes everyone. It also shows that God made that statement because only God knows all people. Step One shows we have sinned.

Step Two

Read Romans 6:23: "For the wages of sin is death, but the gift of God is eternal life in Christ Jesus our Lord." Notice "the wages of sin is death." We have seen in 3:23 that all have sinned. So what? The result is death. Look at wages. This is what a person earns—what one deserves and what one expects to get. So we can all expect to receive death. Look at death. There are two kinds of death. One is physical. Everyone dies—young, old, good, bad, Christians, non-Christians. This is not the death mentioned here. The other is spiritual. This is eternal, horrific, where there will be "weeping and wailing and gnashing of teeth" in an awful place the Bible calls hell. What a horrible fate for the wages of sin. But God does not stop there. The very next words are "but the gift of God is eternal life." Consider the contrast between wages and gift. Wages are what we earn, deserve, and expect. A gift is not earned and probably not expected or deserved.

God loves us and offers us a gift: eternal life. This life is wonderful and joyful, here and now, and we will be forever with God in heaven.

But notice how God gives this gift — "through Jesus Christ our Lord." None of us are perfect. Jesus was perfect. Heaven is a perfect place. All who go there must be perfect. Since Jesus was perfect, and we are not perfect, we need to receive him. He is that free gift God promised. When he comes into our lives, he forgives all our sins and prepares us to go to heaven.

Step Three

A gift that is offered to us does not become ours until we receive it. Read John 1:12: "But as many as received Him, to them He gave the right to become children of God." This verse, along with verse 11, shows that not all people will receive the gift that God has offered. Only those who receive Christ will receive that gift of eternal life.

Some will ask, "How can I receive this gift?"

Step Four

Read Revelation 3:20: "Behold, I stand at the door and knock. If anyone hears My voice and opens the door, I will come in to him." Many people are so busy with other things that they don't hear Jesus knocking. They might hear the knocking but don't want to talk to anyone or be disturbed in what they are doing. Or they might open the door and let that person in. Christ has found us. He wants to come live in us because he loves us. He waits to be invited in. He will not force us to open the door. He wants us to be willing to receive Him.

When Jesus comes into our life, he fulfills the promise: "The gift of God is eternal life."

Step Five

This final step answers the following question: "How can I open the door of my life, my heart?" Read Romans 10:9–10: "That if you confess with your mouth the Lord Jesus and believe in your heart that God raised Him from the dead, you will be saved. For with the heart one believes unto righteousness, and with the mouth confession is made unto salvation."

There are two steps here. Step One: Believe in your heart that Jesus died on a cross for you and that he was raised from the dead. Do you believe that? If so, you have taken the first step. Step Two: Confess with your mouth Jesus is Lord. You simply say a sincere prayer telling God you believe Jesus died for you and that he was raised from the dead. Then ask Jesus to come into your life. Then accept his promise: "You shall be saved."

Remember the two promises in these last two verses. Jesus said, "I will come in," not *might* come in. Here "You will be saved," not *might* be saved.

If you are sincere in asking Jesus to come into your life, you will be saved, then and there. If you are not sincere, God will know this.

You may or may not have wonderful feelings. Just remember feelings come and go, and circumstances can influence how we feel. God's Word never changes. His Word is always trustworthy.

I am grateful that God has blessed me and guided me every step of the way—from the cotton fields of Mississippi, through school, in the churches I pastored, and in ministry at the association and the state convention.

God has blessed me with a wonderful family. They are among my greatest treasures. I have lived a full life with my beautiful wife of nearly seventy years, our three wonderful children, and our amazing grandchildren.

My support group: Jim, Montez, James, Eric, and Dianne.

Printed in the United States
by Baker & Taylor Publisher Services